HIKING

FOR FUN!

By Jef Wilson

Content Adviser: Gary Rutz, U.S. Geological Survey, Cook, Washington
Reading Adviser: Frances Bonacci, Ed.D., Reading Specialist, Cambridge, Massachusetts

COMPASS POINT BOOKS

MINNEAPOLIS, MINNESOTA

Compass Point Books
3109 West 50th Street, #115
Minneapolis, MN 55410

Visit Compass Point Books on the Internet at www.compasspointbooks.com
or e-mail your request to custserv@compasspointbooks.com

Photographs ©: Corbis, front cover, 22-23 (left), 26-27 (left); Photos.com, 4-5, 24-25 (center); Photodisc, 7 (left), 13 (right), 22-23 (center, right), 25, 28 (bottom), 30-31, 42 (top), 42-43 (background), 43 (right), 44 (right); Corel, 7 (right), 21, 27, 35, 42 (center and bottom), 43 (left), 45; AP Wide World Photos, 9, 12-13, 38-39, 40; Comstock, 11 (top, top center), 28 (right); Photos.com 11 (bottom center); Ingram Publishing 10, 11 (bottom), 25 (top); Shutterstock, 14-15; Tom Stewart/Corbis, 16-17, 29; Richard Hutchings/Corbis, 18-19; Eyewire, 28 (top and center); Phil Schermeister/Corbis, 33; Ashley Cooper/Corbis, 37–38; Courtesy of Karen Berger, 41; Ronnie Kaufman/Corbis, 44 (left); Istockphoto, 47.

Editors: Deb Berry and Aubrey Whitten/Bill SMITH STUDIO; and Shelly Lyons
Designer/Page Production: Geron Hoy, Kavita Ramchandran, Sinae Sohn, Marina Terletsky, and Brock Waldron/Bill SMITH STUDIO
Photo Researcher: Jacqueline Lissy Brustein, Scott Rosen, and Allison Smith/Bill SMITH STUDIO
Art Director: Jaime Martens
Creative Director: Keith Griffin
Editorial Director: Carol Jones
Managing Editor: Catherine Neitge

Library of Congress Cataloging-in-Publication Data
Wilson, Jef, 1973-
  Hiking for fun! / by Jef Wilson.
     p. cm. -- (For fun!)
  Includes bibliographical references and index.
  ISBN 0-7565-1686-2 (hard cover)
  1. Hiking--Juvenile literature. I. Title. II. Series.
  GV199.52.W55 2006
  796.51--dc22
                        2005030281

Printed in the United States of America.

Table of Contents

Note: In this book, there are two kinds of vocabulary words. Hiking Words to Know are words specific to hiking. They are defined on page 46. Other Words to Know are helpful words that aren't related only to hiking. They are defined on page 47.

Getting Back to Nature

Hiking, which is exploring the outdoors on foot, is one of the best ways to get connected to nature. It's basically walking or climbing on nature routes or trails. Sometimes there is a special destination, but often the reward of hiking is the walk itself and everything you see along the way—trees, plants, animals, and bodies of water. For many people, it's a great way to "get away from it all."

Once you've mastered the basics of hiking, you might even want to move on to orienteering, a competition in which hikers navigate their way across an area of land. Orienteering will really put your hiking skills to the challenge!

Exploring New Territory

Today, we can easily find out about a place on the other side of the world through encyclopedias, the Internet, and maps. But before there were maps of the whole world, people only knew about the areas close to them. Hiking explorers were the first to find out about other lands.

An ancient Egyptian explorer named Hannu (also known as Hennu) made the first recorded expedition, or trip, around 2750 B.C. Hannu wrote about his explorations in stone. He explored areas that are now part of eastern Ethiopia and Somalia. When he returned to Egypt, he brought back great treasures including metal, wood, and precious myrrh, which is dried tree sap used in perfumes.

Many hikers, trailblazers, and other explorers have charted the world since Hannu. Their efforts have helped people learn all the things we know about the world today.

Lewis and Clark's Adventures

The Lewis and Clark expedition, from 1804 to 1806, was the first trip to the Pacific Coast and back. In the early 1800s, most of the country was uncharted, and people knew very little about it. Lewis and Clark made maps of major rivers and mountain ranges.

A Hike for Everyone!

Hiking allows all kinds of people to enjoy nature. Boys and girls, men and women, young folks and seniors—hiking is for everyone. When you hike, you set your own pace and control where and how you go.

Why hike? Hiking allows you to go places that often cannot be seen any other way. Most hiking trails do not allow cars and bikes, so the only way to enjoy them is by your own two feet. Most hikers also find peace in nature. It can help you relax and relieve stress.

Because of its wide appeal, hiking is a great way to spend time with your family and friends. There are different types of hiking. Off-trail hiking is called "bushwalking" or "bushwhacking." Overnight or longer hikes are called "backpacking." Hiking even has other names in different parts of the world. New Zealanders use the word "tramping" for overnight trips. Hiking in the mountains of Nepal and India is called "trekking."

Exercise Your Rights

Besides being fun, hiking is great exercise! Regular hiking builds strong muscles, a strong heart, and healthy lungs. It builds stamina and endurance, which means you'll have more energy for longer periods of time!

The Bare Essentials

Short hikes over familiar mild trails are easy. For these you only need basics like water, the right footwear, and proper clothes. In general, the longer and more complicated the hike, the more equipment you need to bring. Carefully choose your equipment. Remember that you must carry everything you need and equipment can be heavy.

Never hike without a compass and a map, no matter how well you think you know the area.

Always carry water and water purification tablets in case you have to refill your bottles from a stream.

The footwear you'll need for your hike depends on the terrain. For very clean, cleared trails, you might even be able to hike in cross-trainers. But for more difficult routes, a pair of good hiking boots is a must.

Magnify It!
Binoculars are a great way to observe animals and plants without getting too close. A pair that magnifies by seven or eight power is perfect for hiking.

The Right Fit

Before dressing for your hike, answer these questions: What kind of trail will you hike? Will you be hiking on or off trail? At what altitude will you hike? Will you be hiking in different altitudes, like going up and down a mountain? In what season and in what weather will you hike?

It's best to dress in layers so you can adjust them as needed. There are three main layers. The first is the wicking layer, which wicks or pulls perspiration away from the skin toward the next layer of clothing, where it evaporates. The second is the insulation layer. This layer keeps you warm. The last layer is the shell. The shell protects you from elements like rain, snow, sleet, or bright sun.

In the past, hikers relied on natural materials like wool and cotton. Today's hikers have discovered that synthetic, or man-made, materials work better. There are different kinds of synthetics, and none of them hold moisture like wool and cotton can.

These Boots Are Made for Hiking!

The best hiking boots are sturdy, fit well, and are waterproof. Most hiking boots are of fabric-leather-and-rubber construction. Boots for hiking usually have nonskid rubber soles that are good for many types of terrain, from slippery wet rocks to sand or mud.

13

Taking Your First Steps

You can advance from short walks to longer trail hikes. One way is to learn from an expert. If you don't know any experts, try joining an outdoors club in your area. This is a great way to meet other people who like to hike.

Taking a guided hike is an excellent way to learn all kinds of things to make you a better hiker. Taking classes can also help.

State and regional parks and stores that sell hiking gear often have information about group activities and hikes, and they sometimes even offer classes and workshops.

Start Here

The best way to learn is to just get out there and hike! Start with shorter easy or "novice" rated trails and work your way up. This will help you build your skills and improve your physical abilities a little at a time.

Happy Trails to You!

Hiking trails can be either marked or unmarked. Marked trails have numbers or names ("signs" or "blazes") painted onto rocks and trees at forks and other locations, and they are more likely to be maintained. This means the paths get cleared of brush and fallen trees.

Marked trails are rated by difficulty. Whether easy, moderate, or difficult depends on the length and how steep or rugged the terrain is. Sometimes trails are rated novice, intermediate, or expert. Expert trails may have natural obstacles like shallow stream crossings or very narrow paths along high ridges.

Unmarked trails can be more difficult to hike and navigate. They are not for beginners. These trails may have originally been made by animals or can be old, abandoned hunting or hiking trails. They are not cleared and can have many obstacles, some of which are dangerous.

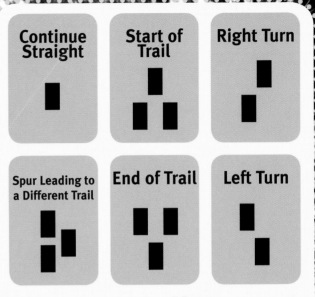

Continue Straight	Start of Trail	Right Turn
▮	▮ ▮▮	▮ ▮

Spur Leading to a Different Trail	End of Trail	Left Turn
▮ ▮	▮ ▮ ▮	▮ ▮

What Does It All Mean?

Here are some common symbols used on trails. Often, turn signals don't show a left or right direction. One blaze is simply painted directly above the other.

The Lay of the Land

Hikers should always have the basic tools of navigation: a compass and maps. Knowledge of the area is also necessary. Knowing the locations of natural landmarks like streams, rivers, and mountains is very important.

Maps provide the directions you need, and the compass is the tool that helps you follow them. A compass needle always points to magnetic north, which is the North Pole.

Topographic maps are best for navigating areas off the beaten path. Unlike a road map, topographic maps show whether the land is flat, mountainous, steep, or rocky. High and low spots are shown by using contour lines.

Walking a Fine Line

Contour lines are lines on a map that connect points of equal elevation, or height. Lines that are close together show elevation change. Lines farther apart show very little change in elevation. When the contour lines cross, you'll find an abrupt drop, like a canyon or maybe even a waterfall.

Flora and Fauna

Recognizing different plants and animals will enhance your hiking experience and help you stay safe. Look for park brochures and hiking guides to learn about the types of flora and fauna in your region.

Flora is another name for plant life. Some types of flora include coniferous (cone-bearing) trees, deciduous trees (trees that grow and lose their leaves each season), flowers, ferns, mosses, algae, and fungi. Each type of plant has traits to identify it. You can identify a tree by its shape, leaves, needles, or cones it produces.

Fauna is another word for animal life. One of the greatest benefits of hiking is the chance to see wild animals in their own habitats. You might see creatures like deer, rabbits, or lizards. Other commonly seen animals include squirrels, chipmunks, rabbits, birds, and reptiles.

Creepy, Crawly, and Contagious!

Certain plants, animals, and insects can ruin your hike. The best defense is to know which plants, animals, and insects live in the areas you hike and how to avoid the harmful ones.

Poison ivy, poison oak, and poison sumac are closely related, and touching any of them can cause an itchy or painful rash.

Bites from insects like mosquitoes are mostly a nuisance, leaving itchy or burning bites. But some insect bites can make you very sick. For instance, a bite from a brown recluse spider will likely need immediate treatment.

Make sure you know how to spot poisonous snakes in the area you plan to hike. A bite from a poisonous snake needs immediate treatment, so you should never hike without a snakebite kit. If you are ever bitten by a snake, get immediate medical attention.

Cute but Not Cuddly!

That raccoon might be adorable, but don't try to pet or feed it. Raccoons are a common animal spotted on hikes, but they have been known to attack and bite. Some raccoons also carry rabies, a disease that affects the nervous system and can be fatal if left untreated.

Walking Farther, Climbing Higher

For very simple hikes, you might go out for a few hours in nothing but a T-shirt, shorts, and boots. More serious hikes require a lot more equipment and supplies, especially in the event that you meet up with the unexpected. You might get stuck in bad weather, hit an obstacle you can't get around, or even get lost! This is where backpacking comes into play.

Backpackers try to keep the weight and bulk of their gear as low as they can. A lighter load causes less chance for injury. By traveling light, you can go longer distances.

In the 1930s, a hiking, climbing, and conservation organization called the Mountaineers came up with a list of 10 essential items that should always be in your backpack. The list has since been updated by modern hikers.

Ten Things to Keep in Your Backpack

• map

• compass

• water and a way to purify it

• extra food

• rain gear and extra clothing

• flashlight and extra batteries

• pocketknife or multipurpose tool

• first aid kit

• fire starter and matches

• sunscreen and sunglasses

Sleeping Bags and S'mores!

A hike can last as long as you want it to or as long as your supplies last. Some hikers only go out for a few hours, while others make it an adventure that can last days or even weeks. For those longer hikes, you'll need to set up campsites so you can sleep, rest, and eat along the way.

If you plan to set up camp, you should have all the same essentials for backpacking. The other basics you'll need are a tent, sleeping bags, and a way to build fires for warmth or cooking. Some good campfire songs and ghost stories to tell around the fire are great to have, too. Also, don't forget to bring the marshmallows and ingredients for s'mores!

Campfire Safety

The first rule is: Never leave a campfire unattended! Build your fire in a pit with plenty of rocks around it to contain stray flames. Make sure there are no branches or dry brush near the fire, and keep a bucket of water nearby. When leaving the campsite, fully extinguish the fire with water or by smothering it with dirt or sand.

Don't Get Stung!

When you're out in the woods or high up in a mountain, any number of things can go wrong. Access to immediate, professional medical attention probably won't be available. That's why you should never go on an extended hike without a first aid kit and basic knowledge of first aid.

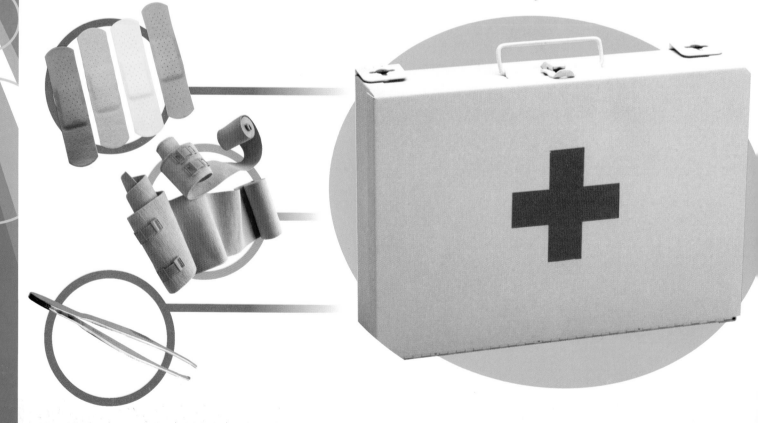

What Should Be in Your First Aid Kit?

- sunscreen

- pain relief tablets such as ibuprofen

- butterfly closure bandages

- gauze bandages

- water purification tablets

- antiseptics such as hydrogen peroxide, iodine, or Betadine

- antibacterial ointment such as Neosporin

- tourniquet

- Vaseline or similar petroleum jelly

- snakebite kit

- tweezers for splinters

- anti-itch cream or calamine lotion

- adhesive bandages in various sizes

- gauze compress pads

- moleskin to apply to blister-prone areas as a treatment or preventive measure

First Aid Classes
Take a basic first aid class with the American Red Cross or a wilderness first aid class offered by many hiking organizations.

The Law of the Land

Hikers look for beautiful places. Sometimes these environments are fragile. Hikers could accidentally damage them. The actions of one hiker may not cause much damage, but imagine what a large number of careless hikers could do.

State parks or protected areas have regulations in place to protect the environment. These rules cover things like where to get firewood or whether fires are even allowed. Hikers should always follow these rules.

No matter where you hike, follow the rule of "Leave No Trace." This means hiking in a way that hikers after you cannot tell you were ever there.

Public Lands

The Bureau of Land Management (BLM) is an agency within the U.S. Department of the Interior. It looks after public lands. These lands total 262 million acres (104.8 million hectares) or one-eighth of the whole country!

WARNING

NO DUMPING ALLOWED

VIOLATORS WILL BE PROSECUTED

REDWOOD CITY MUNI CODE SEC. 14.5

$500 FINE

Hiking with a Twist

Orienteering is a competition where hikers navigate from one point to another through unfamiliar territory. Competitors use their hiking and navigation skills to race to the end. Most hikers use maps and a compass to find their way. Sometimes there are special instructions about things to do or pick up along the way. In many ways it is like a scavenger hunt in the woods!

Typically, orienteer participants are given a map of an area that shows several sites to visit. They find the quickest route to the locations and prove they visited each one.

In many orienteering events, you carry a special card. At each location, someone punches your card as proof that you were there.

Thinking Together

There are special orienteering events. These are designed around doing a special activity, solving a problem, answering a question, or retrieving a special object. The only limit to the type of event is your imagination!

Mountain High, Valley Low

There are many hiking trails in the United States, but three stand out. Because of their length and the large differences in landscape from beginning to end, hikers call these trails the Triple Crown. Hikers of the Triple Crown wind through some of the most amazing scenery in the United States.

First is the Appalachian Trail. It crosses the tops of several of the Appalachian Mountains, running almost continuously through the wilderness.

The rugged Pacific Crest Trail crosses more challenging terrain at higher altitudes. Highlights include the Sonoran and Mojave deserts and the Sierra Nevada and Cascade mountain ranges from Mexico to Canada.

The Continental Divide Trail provides amazing travel of the length of the Rocky Mountains from Mexico to Canada. Highlights include Glacier National Park, Yellowstone National Park, and the Great Divide Basin.

Appalachian Trail
- Length: 2,160 miles (3,456 kilometers)
- Route: Ridgelines of the Appalachian Mountains

Pacific Crest Trail
- Length: 2,655 miles (4,248 km)
- Route: Crest of the Sierra Nevada and Cascade mountain ranges, from Mexico to Canada

Continental Divide Trail
- Length: 3,100 miles (4,960 km)
- Route: Crest of the Rocky Mountains

No Mountain High Enough

Hiking can open the door to many other nature activities. Mountain climbing is also called mountaineering. In Europe it is called alpinism. Mountain climbing is divided into two types: rock-craft and snow-craft, depending on whether the mountaineer chooses a route over rock or over snow and ice. Both require great gymnastic and technical ability. Experience is also important, especially for snow-craft, which is dangerous.

Caving, also called spelunking, is the exploration of caves by foot. While caving can be exciting, it can also be dangerous and requires great physical ability. When caving, you'll often have to crawl through tight areas or use ropes to get from one part of a cave to another. Keep in mind, mountain climbing and caving are dangerous activities and should only be attempted by experienced hikers. They should also never be attempted while you are alone.

Rock climbers scale the faces of large rock outcroppings. Often these outcroppings have nearly vertical grades. Rock climbers use their hands and feet to find holds in the rock. Aid-climbers use special equipment to help them climb. Free-climbers climb without equipment to help them. They only use ropes or protective gear in case of a fall.

Giving Back

Keeping trails in good condition is called trail maintenance. Weather and other factors can destroy trails. They need people to keep them in good shape. Without trail maintenance, you would have a lot fewer miles of trail to hike. There would be a lot more fallen trees, bogs, mud puddles, prickly plants, and poison ivy, too.

Many parks have a trail crew, people who are paid to maintain trails. However, there are always more trails than the parks can afford to maintain. This is where volunteers come in!

Volunteers do the same things as the trail crew, like clipping branches, sawing through blown-down trees, and making drainage ditches to drain bogs.

The rewards of volunteering include meeting other hikers, developing new outdoor skills, and achieving the good feeling of giving back to nature and other hikers. To help in your area, contact your local parks department and ask them how you can get involved. Many parks sponsor events like volunteer trail work weekends.

Then and Now

In 1953 Edmund P. Hillary and Sardar Tenzing Norgay climbed to the summit of Mount Everest for the first time. Mount Everest is the largest mountain in the world. At 29,028 feet (8,854 meters), its summit is the highest place on Earth.

Edmund Hillary was a professional beekeeper from New Zealand. Tenzing Norgay was a professional mountaineer from the Sherpa community of the Everest foothills, Nepal.

Being the first made them famous throughout the world. *Time* magazine named them among the 20 most "influential heroes and icons of the 20th century." Within 20 years of their climb, hundreds of people followed in their footsteps to reach the summit.

KAREN BERGER

Karen Berger is a modern day hiker. She has finished the Appalachian, Pacific Crest, and Continental Divide trails. This makes her one of the few who have completed hiking's Triple Crown, which is all three of these long distance trails. Over the last 10 years, Berger has hiked more than 15,000 miles (24,000 km) on five continents!

Karen is a full time writer. She collaborates with her husband Daniel R. Smith to write books about her many hiking adventures and her love of animals. She currently lives in Great Barrington, Massachusetts.

What Happened When?

2750 B.C.   **1800 A.D.**   **1900**   **1910**   **1920**   **1930**

2750 Hannu, an ancient Egyptian explorer, makes the first recorded exploring expedition.

1804 to 1806 Explorers Lewis and Clark make the first expedition to the Pacific Coast and back.

1920s to 1930s The Appalachian Trail is designed, constructed, and marked by volunteer hiking clubs.

1889 Hans Meyer of Germany and Ludwig Purtscheller of Austria become the first to scale Kilimanjaro, the highest mountain in Africa.

1271 to 1295 Marco Polo makes his famous travels throughout Asia.

1913 Hudson Stuck leads the first climb of Mount McKinley in Alaska.

1513 Juan Ponce de León is regarded as the first European to visit what is the present day United States when he sets foot on Florida soil.

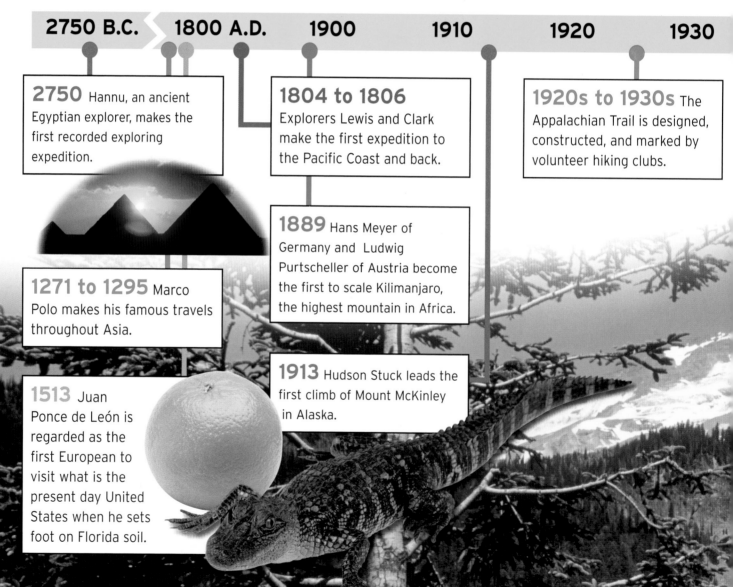

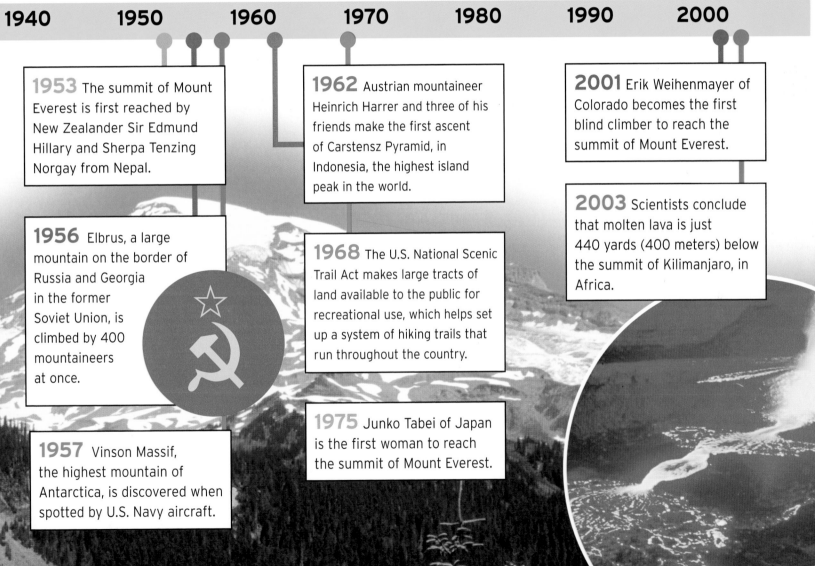

1940   **1950**   **1960**   **1970**   **1980**   **1990**   **2000**

1953 The summit of Mount Everest is first reached by New Zealander Sir Edmund Hillary and Sherpa Tenzing Norgay from Nepal.

1956 Elbrus, a large mountain on the border of Russia and Georgia in the former Soviet Union, is climbed by 400 mountaineers at once.

1957 Vinson Massif, the highest mountain of Antarctica, is discovered when spotted by U.S. Navy aircraft.

1962 Austrian mountaineer Heinrich Harrer and three of his friends make the first ascent of Carstensz Pyramid, in Indonesia, the highest island peak in the world.

1968 The U.S. National Scenic Trail Act makes large tracts of land available to the public for recreational use, which helps set up a system of hiking trails that run throughout the country.

1975 Junko Tabei of Japan is the first woman to reach the summit of Mount Everest.

2001 Erik Weihenmayer of Colorado becomes the first blind climber to reach the summit of Mount Everest.

2003 Scientists conclude that molten lava is just 440 yards (400 meters) below the summit of Kilimanjaro, in Africa.

Fun Hiking Facts

The Appalachian Trail starts in Georgia and continues through South Carolina, North Carolina, Tennessee, Virginia, Maryland, Pennsylvania, New York, New Jersey, and ends in Maine.

The average person walks 114,332 miles (182,931 km) during his or her lifetime!

Eight thousand years ago, the Earth was covered by approximately 14.8 billion acres (5.9 billion hectares) of forests. Today the world's forest area has shrunk to 8.6 billion acres (3.4 billion hectares).

The Wrangell-St. Elias National Park and Preserve in Alaska covers 13.2 million acres (5.3 billion hectares).

During Lewis and Clark's explorations of what became the United States, they discovered and described 178 new plants and 122 species and subspecies of animals.

llowstone National Park, which spreads ross parts of Wyoming, Idaho, and Montana, the oldest national park in the world. It has ore than 1,100 miles (1,760 km) of hiking ils and is a great place to enjoy nature.

According to the American Hiking Society, about one-third of Americans went hiking in the U.S. in 2002.

Hiking Words to Know

altitude: the height of a thing above sea level or above Earth's surface

brush: growth of bushes or shrubs

bushwalking: Australian word for hiking or backpacking

charted: areas of land that have been discovered and studied

compass: a device used to find geographic direction using a magnetic needle that uses Earth's magnetic field to point north

coniferous: any tree or plant that produces cones

deciduous: trees that shed or lose leaves at the end of the season

elevation: distance of something above a reference point (such as sea level)

expedition: a group journey with a definite objective such as exploration

fauna: animals, especially of a certain region

flora: plants, especially of a certain region

fork: a single trail that splits into two

landmark: any feature of a place or terrain that stands out

magnetic north: the direction a compass needle points, using Earth's magnetic field

mountaineer: one who climbs mountains for sport

navigate: to follow a planned course on, across, or through

orienteering: a cross-country race in which competitors use a map and compass to find their way through unfamiliar territory

outfitter: any retailer that sells clothing or outerwear for outdoor use

scavenger hunt: a game in which individuals or teams try to find miscellaneous items on a list

shell: outer layer of clothing, such as a jacket, that protects you from the elements like rain, snow, sleet, or sun

terrain: a piece of ground having specific features

trail: a marked or worn path through woods or wilderness

trail blazer: one who creates and marks trails

trail crew: group of people who maintain trails

tramping: New Zealand word for a hiking trip, especially an overnight trip

trekking: hiking in the mountainous regions of Nepal and India

wicking: a layer of fabric that pulls perspiration away from the skin toward the next layer of clothing

Metric Conversion
1 yard = .9144 meters

Other Words to Know

aerobic: type of exercise that helps respiratory and circulatory systems

destination: the place to which one is going or directed

durable: capable of withstanding wear and tear without showing signs of damage or wear

endurance: the act, quality, or power of withstanding strenuous activity

enthusiast: one who has an interest in a specific activity or hobby

essential: very important, necessary

fragile: incapable of withstanding wear and tear without showing signs of damage or wear

inaccessible: capable of being reached only with great difficulty or not at all

obstacle: anything that stands in the way of or holds up progress

purify: to make pure by removing any other material such as dirt or bacteria

scenery: a view or views of natural features, especially in open country

stamina: the strength to resist or withstand illness, fatigue, or hardship; endurance

synthetic: not of natural origin; prepared or made artificially

workshop: organized event where a skill is learned

Where To Learn More

AT THE LIBRARY

Berger, Karen. *Trailside Guide: Hiking and Backpacking*. New York: W. W. Norton & Company, 2003.

Hall, Adrienne. *Basic Essentials Backpacking*. Old Saybrook, Conn.: Globe Pequot, 1999.

Werner, Doug. *Backpacker's Start-Up: A Beginner's Guide to Hiking & Backpacking*. Chula Vista, Calif.: Tracks Publishing, 1999.

ON THE ROAD

Saguaro National Park
2700 North Kinney Road
Tuscan, AZ 85743

ON THE WEB

For more information on HIKING, use FactHound to track down Web sites related to this book.

1. Go to www.facthound.com
2. Type in this book ID: 0756516862
3. Click on the *Fetch It* button.

Your trusty FactHound will fetch the best Web sites for you!

INDEX

ABOUT THE AUTHOR

Jef Wilson grew up in Missouri where he enjoyed many outdoor nature activities, including hiking, camping, and hunting. Throughout North America, he has explored a variety of trails and landscapes by foot or by bicycle. He is currently a writer and illustrator in educational publishing. He lives in New Jersey where he continues to enjoy and explore the great outdoors with his two young sons, Arlo and Cage.